INVENTIONS IN 30 SECONDS

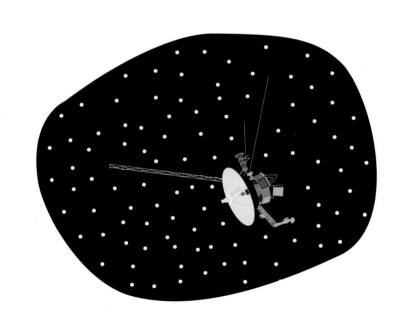

First published in the UK in 2014 by Ivy Kids.
This edition published in the US in 2017 by

Ivy Kids

Ovest House
58 West Street
Brighton BN1 2RA
United Kingdom
www.quartoknows.com

A CIP record for this book is available from the Library of Congress.

ISBN: 978-1-78240-485-9

This book was conceived, designed & produced by

Ivy Kids

PUBLISHER	Susan Kelly
CREATIVE DIRECTOR	Peter Bridgewater
COMMISSIONING EDITOR	Hazel Songhurst
PROJECT EDITOR	Claire Saunders
ART DIRECTOR	Kim Hankinson
DESIGNERS	Amy McSimpson
	and Lisa McCormick
ILLUSTRATOR	Marta Munoz

Printed in China

10 9 8 7 6 5 4 3 2 1

INVENTIONS
IN 30 SECONDS

DR MIKE GOLDSMITH

ILLUSTRATED BY CHRIS ANDERSON

IVY KIDS

Contents

About this book
... in 60 seconds

Look around you: how many inventions can you count?
Chances are, there are hundreds—and life wouldn't be
the same without them.

Almost everything around us is only there because somebody,
somewhere, saw that there was a need for it—and invented it. Think
about it—you are only reading these words today because hundreds
of years ago somebody invented the printing press, and before that
other people invented paper and ink... and even writing itself.

Who invented these things? When we think of an inventor it's
easy to imagine someone with wild hair working alone in a
laboratory full of crazy gizmos—and some inventors have come
up with their ideas just like that. But usually, inventions are
developed by many people over a long time. Sometimes
it takes hundreds of years and several different inventors
to get from the original bright idea to a final version
that actually does the job.

Until a century or two ago, a big problem for inventors was that their ideas were often stolen by other people. Thankfully, someone invented an invention to make inventors happier—the patent. When you patent an invention, an organization called the patent office has the job of checking that your creation hasn't already been invented, and then making sure that no one copies your idea.

One thing that makes a great inventor different from a great scientist, mathematician, or engineer is that they don't need to spend years at school, college, or university. Many inventors just had a great idea and followed it up. So, anyone can be an inventor, including you!

This book explores 30 of the world's best inventions. Each has a one-page history of the invention and a speedy sum-up if you're short on time. Then you can try out the missions—make a compass, create electricity, measure a microwave, power a rocket, invent a superhuman implant, and more!

Making life easy

Many inventions have come about just to make life easier for us. In ancient times, people would simply adapt what nature provided, making rough shelters from branches, and using hollow shells for cups and animal skins for clothes. Gradually, inventions such as weaving, the flushing toilet, central heating, and electric light made our lives easier and more comfortable, and today most of us take them completely for granted.

Making life easy
Glossary

abacus A device that helps people calculate sums by storing numbers.

biodegradable Able to break down naturally and in a way that is not harmful to plants and animals.

boiler A water heater, often with pipes and a pump to send the heated water where it is needed.

chamber pot A container for bodily waste, before flushing toilets were in common use.

energy The power that makes other things happen. Electricity, radioactivity, heat, light, and sound are all kinds of energy.

fabric A soft material, such as woven cotton, made in sheets.

filament A fine wire that glows brightly when electricity is passed through it.

fluorescent bulb A gas-filled light bulb. Its inner surface glows when electricity is present.

flax A type of grass-like plant from which linen is made.

furnace A place where fuel is burned, often to provide the heat for a building.

germ A tiny living thing or a complicated chemical, too small to see without a microscope, that causes diseases.

incandescent bulb A light bulb that contains a **filament**.

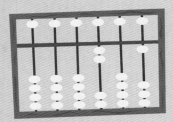 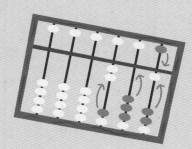 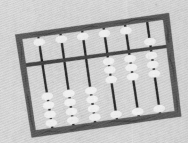

Industrial Revolution The period beginning in the late 18th century, when steam power changed the world by improving transport and the way goods were made.

insulated Covered with a material that prevents heat or electricity from escaping.

lagging Material used to cover a hot water pipe or tank to keep in the heat.

linen Probably the oldest kind of fabric, made from **flax**. It is still used today.

loom A machine that weaves thread into fabric.

nylon One of the earliest artificial fibers, originally used mainly to replace silk.

petroleum A liquid found underground, used as a fuel or as an ingredient in making things, such as plastics.

sewer A tunnel, ditch, or pipe used to carry bodily waste and rainwater away.

thermostat A type of automatic switch that is triggered when a particular temperature is reached. A thermostat is often used to switch on a heating system when a room gets cold enough to need it.

warp thread The thread that is strung across the length of a loom. The **weft thread** is passed over and under the **warp thread** to make woven fabric.

weft thread The thread that is passed over and under the **warp threads**, across the width of the loom, to make woven fabric.

Weaving

... in 30 seconds

Clothes, blankets, towels, curtains, carpets—it's hard to imagine life without them. But for thousands of years, all that humans had to wear and sleep under were the skins of animals.

Then, about 6,000 years ago, someone discovered that the fibers of certain plants and animal fleeces could be twisted and spun to form long, strong strands, or yarn. The very first yarn was probably linen, which is made from a reed-like plant called flax. Later, the fluffy coverings of the seeds of cotton plants and the equally fluffy coats of sheep were used to make strands of cotton and wool.

But, how could people make clothes and other useful things from these strands? By weaving! The first looms (weaving machines) were probably invented in Ancient Egypt, and the idea spread all over the world. In the 18th century, people put many big looms together in some of the first factories. In the 19th century, steam power was used to operate much larger looms. In the 20th century, electrical power took over and it is still used today.

3-second sum-up

Weaving turns threads into fabric.

3-minute mission Weaving

You need: 2 sheets of colored paper, one paler than the other • scissors • white glue

Cut 12 strips of paper ½ x 6 in (1 x 12 cm) in one color, and 12 strips in the second color.

Weave the strips over and under, gluing down the ends as you go, to make a square. Try making other shapes or using four colors. What happens if the paler strips are thinner?

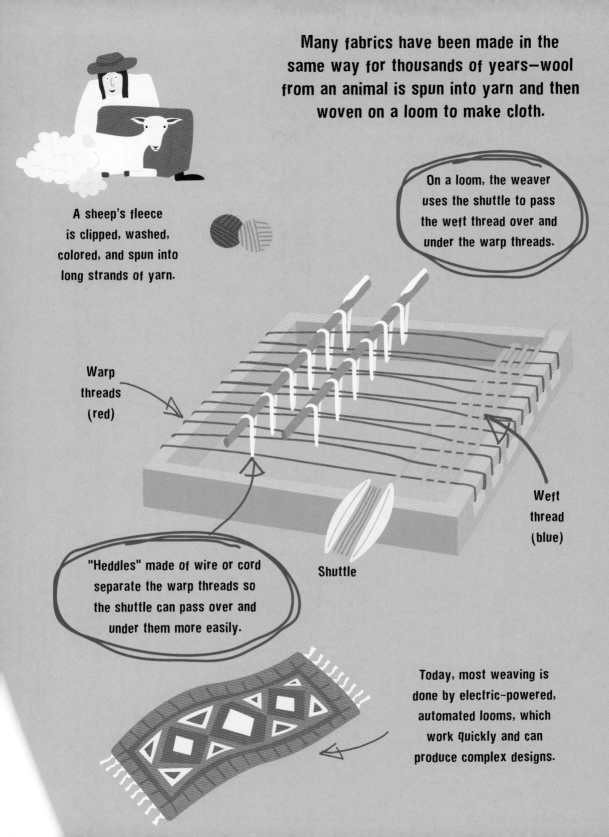

Many fabrics have been made in the same way for thousands of years—wool from an animal is spun into yarn and then woven on a loom to make cloth.

A sheep's fleece is clipped, washed, colored, and spun into long strands of yarn.

On a loom, the weaver uses the shuttle to pass the weft thread over and under the warp threads.

Warp threads (red)

Weft thread (blue)

"Heddles" made of wire or cord separate the warp threads so the shuttle can pass over and under them more easily.

Shuttle

Today, most weaving is done by electric-powered, automated looms, which work quickly and can produce complex designs.

Abacus

... in 30 seconds

Ever since people have had things to count or trade, they have needed mathematics. While simple sums can be done in your head or on your fingers, bigger numbers need something more—introducing the abacus.

The first abacus was probably just a few grooves in the sand. Each groove stood for something different: the first groove might have meant "hundreds", the second "tens," and the third "ones." By placing stones in the grooves, numbers could be recorded; by moving them around, sums could be calculated.

The abacus that we know today—beads that slide on rods in a wooden frame—was invented in China over 2,000 years ago. The abacus continued to be used for thousands of years, and can still be found in some places today. The abacus was the first of many mathematical inventions, including the mechanical calculator (invented in the 17th century), the electronic calculator (used from the 1970s), and the computer.

3-second sum-up

The abacus was the first invention to make sums simple.

3-minute mission Make an abacus

You need: A rectangle of stiff cardboard, about 8 x 12 inches (30 cm x 20 cm) • Six 8-inch (20 cm) lengths of string • 30 beads • Adhesive tape • A ruler

Cut out the center of the card to make a frame. Thread five beads on each string and tape one end to the bottom of the frame and the other end to the top. Slide the first four beads of each string to the bottom and the other bead to the top. Then tape the ruler across the frame so that it separates the groups of beads.

An abacus counts in ones and fives. Beads above the horizontal beam are fives (5s); beads below the beam are singles (1s).

To read a column, count the number of 1s and 5s that are touching the beam. So, this abacus is storing 1,352,964,709.

5s

Beam

1s (singles)

Billions Hundred millions Ten millions Millions Hundred thousands Ten thousands Thousands Hundreds Tens Ones

The abacus was used by traders for thousands of years. Here it is shown adding numbers, but it could also subtract, divide, and multiply.

137

201

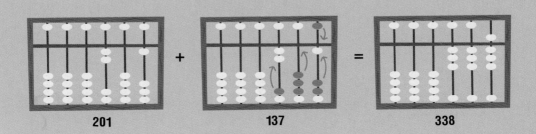

201   +   137   =   338

Central heating

... in 30 seconds

Fifty years ago, central heating (that is, a method of moving heat from a single source through a building) was rare. Electrical or gas heaters, or simple fires, kept people warm instead. Now, in cool climates, nearly every modern home has central heating.

But, strangely, central heating isn't a modern invention—it was invented by the Romans in about 200 BCE. They built their high-class houses with gaps under the floors and behind the walls, and hot air and smoke from a furnace (an enclosed fire) would pass through those gaps on its way outside. This was called a hypocaust.

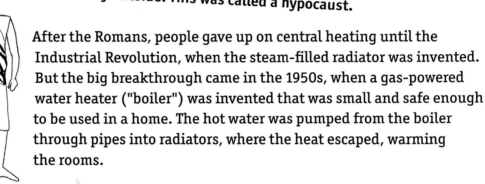

After the Romans, people gave up on central heating until the Industrial Revolution, when the steam-filled radiator was invented. But the big breakthrough came in the 1950s, when a gas-powered water heater ("boiler") was invented that was small and safe enough to be used in a home. The hot water was pumped from the boiler through pipes into radiators, where the heat escaped, warming the rooms.

3-second sum-up

Central heating makes our homes comfier and easier to heat.

3-minute mission Keeping heat in

You need: 2 identical tin cans (or glass jars) with lids • An old sweater • A thermometer

Fill both tin cans or glass jars to the top with very warm water and replace the lids. Wrap one tin in a jumper. After 20 minutes, use a thermometer to test the temperature of both cans. The sweater has "insulated" the wrapped can and helped reduce the loss of heat—just as a material known as "lagging" does on hot-water pipes today. Try other materials like corrugated cardboard, cotton batting or bubble-wrap to see which works best.

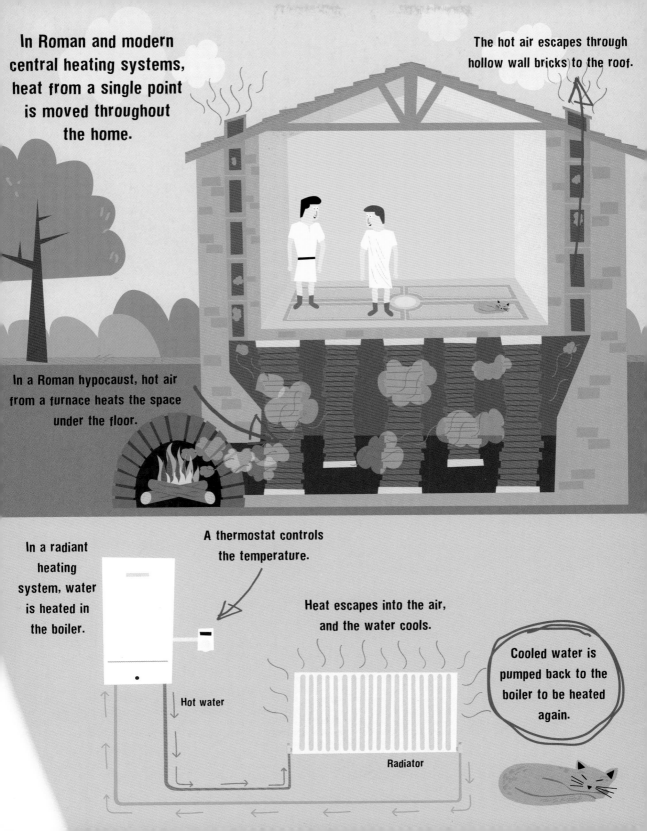

In Roman and modern central heating systems, heat from a single point is moved throughout the home.

The hot air escapes through hollow wall bricks to the roof.

In a Roman hypocaust, hot air from a furnace heats the space under the floor.

In a radiant heating system, water is heated in the boiler.

A thermostat controls the temperature.

Heat escapes into the air, and the water cools.

Cooled water is pumped back to the boiler to be heated again.

Hot water

Radiator

Flushing toilet

... in 30 seconds

Before people started to live in houses, going to the toilet was easy—you just did what you needed to do and then moved on. But going to the toilet in a house raises a problem: what to do with the waste? Rich people had servants to take away their waste-filled "chamber pots", which were emptied into rivers or even just onto the street.

Having a lot of waste around the place wasn't just smelly. Human waste is full of germs of all kinds, many of which are deadly.

In 1597 Queen Elizabeth I became the lucky user of the world's first modern flushing toilet, invented by her godson, Sir John Harington. Sadly it was still smelly, and it didn't solve the problem of getting rid of the waste. In fact, this stayed a problem until the 19th century, when people finally discovered the danger of germs, and insisted on special tunnels called sewers, for toilets to be emptied into.

Sir John's invention was ahead of its time. Only two of his toilets were ever built, and it took almost 200 years for the next flushing toilets to appear.

3-second sum-up

The flushing toilet replaced chamber pots and got rid of germs and smells.

Bottom-wiping

The Chinese have been using paper for bottom-wiping for more than 2,500 years. In other countries and at other times, other materials were used, including snow, stones, sponges on sticks, broken pots, and sea shells—no wonder many preferred to use water. In the 19th century, old newspaper was popular. But in 1857, toilet paper, invented by Joseph C. Gayetty, went on sale in the US.

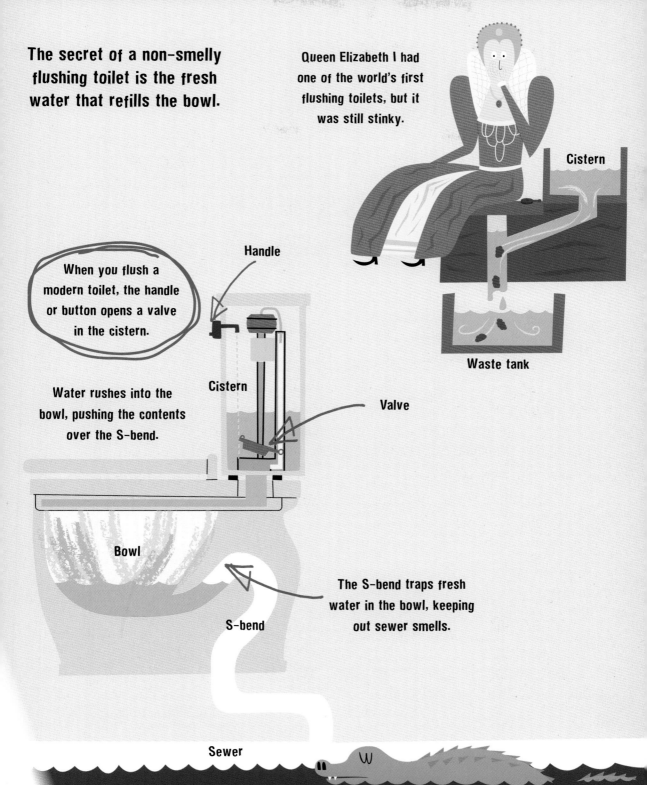

The secret of a non-smelly flushing toilet is the fresh water that refills the bowl.

Queen Elizabeth I had one of the world's first flushing toilets, but it was still stinky.

Cistern

Waste tank

When you flush a modern toilet, the handle or button opens a valve in the cistern.

Handle

Cistern

Valve

Water rushes into the bowl, pushing the contents over the S-bend.

Bowl

The S-bend traps fresh water in the bowl, keeping out sewer smells.

S-bend

Sewer

Light bulb

... in 30 seconds

The light bulb is such a great invention that it's used in cartoons over people's heads when they have a bright idea! And it really did change the world. Before its invention, most people had to rely on gas lamps, candles, or oil lamps to give them light. But the light bulb made homes and businesses light enough to live and work in comfortably after dark—all at the flick of a switch.

The light bulb was perfected by US inventor Thomas Edison in the 1870s. The idea was simple—when electricity passes through a thin wire ("filament") it heats it up enough to glow. The problem was how to prevent the wire from burning away—and the answer was to put it in a bulb from which the air had been removed. No air means no burning and a bulb that lasts.

Now, few bulbs have filaments—they contain special gases instead. These newer bulbs (called fluorescent bulbs) were invented in 1926 and are a vast improvement, because they create less heat and so turn most of the electricity they receive into light.

3-second sum-up

Electricity passing through a thin wire produced heat and light.

3-minute mission Light a bulb

You need: A balloon • A fluorescent bulb • An adult helper

Take the balloon and bulb into a dark room. Rub the balloon quickly against your hair 60 or more times to charge it with static electricity. Touch the balloon to the bulb, and tiny sparks will appear. The sparks come from the static electricity, just as the bulb's usual glow comes from the electrical supply of the house.

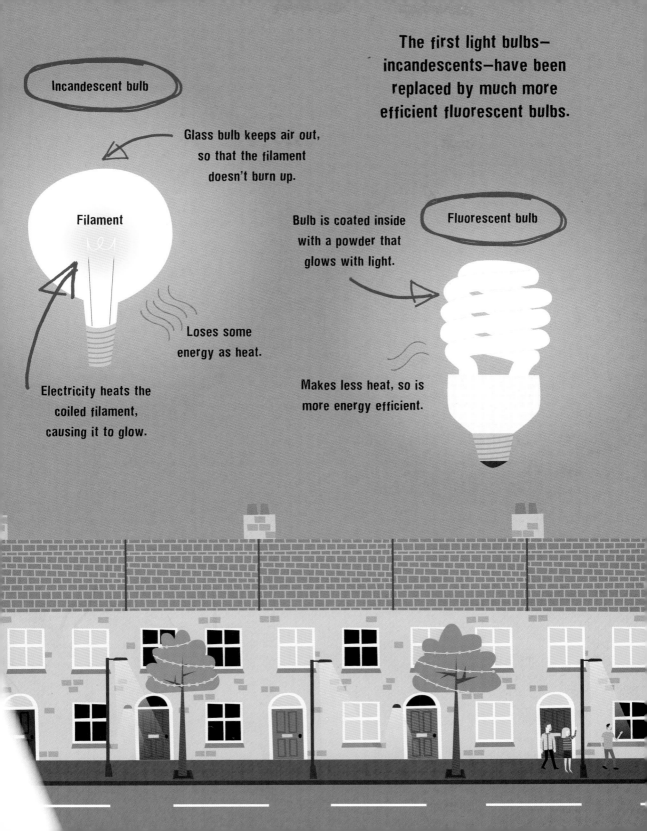

Artificial fiber

... in 30 seconds

Natural fibers such as wool, cotton, and silk are useful in many ways, but they have their limitations. The invention of artificial fibers (that is, fibers made from chemicals rather than animals or plants) meant we could make stronger, cheaper material, and no longer had to rely on fields of cotton or herds of sheep.

One of the earliest, and most important, artificial fibers was nylon, invented by Wallace Carothers in 1935. Carothers set out to make a cheaper alternative to women's delicate and expensive silk stockings. Nylon, made from petroleum, quickly replaced silk in stockings and many other things, including World War II parachutes.

Other artificial fibers soon followed, including polyester in the 1950s (today's most popular artificial fiber), and new fibers are still being invented. Artificial fibers are used to make all sorts of things, not just material. Guitar strings, sieves, bulletproof vests, and even the stitches used in operations (which dissolve after they've done their job) are all made from artificial fibers.

3-second sum-up

Artificial fibers can be used to make things that are stronger and cheaper than natural alternatives.

Natural versus artificial

Are your clothes made from natural fibers such as cotton, wool, or linen, or from artificial fibers such as polyester and nylon? Or perhaps a mix of both? Take a look at the labels to find out.

What's so good about artificial fiber? For starters, it is strong, and quick to dry when it gets wet. It doesn't rely on crops or animals being farmed, and it's cheap to produce and to buy. On the downside, it's not biodegradable, and when it is made, it causes much more pollution than natural fiber does.

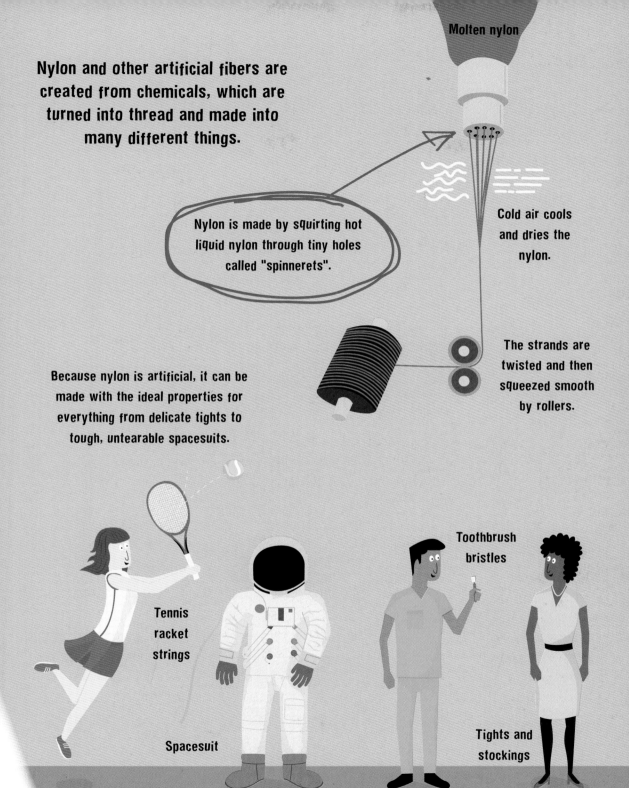

Nylon and other artificial fibers are created from chemicals, which are turned into thread and made into many different things.

Molten nylon

Nylon is made by squirting hot liquid nylon through tiny holes called "spinnerets".

Cold air cools and dries the nylon.

The strands are twisted and then squeezed smooth by rollers.

Because nylon is artificial, it can be made with the ideal properties for everything from delicate tights to tough, untearable spacesuits.

Tennis racket strings

Spacesuit

Toothbrush bristles

Tights and stockings

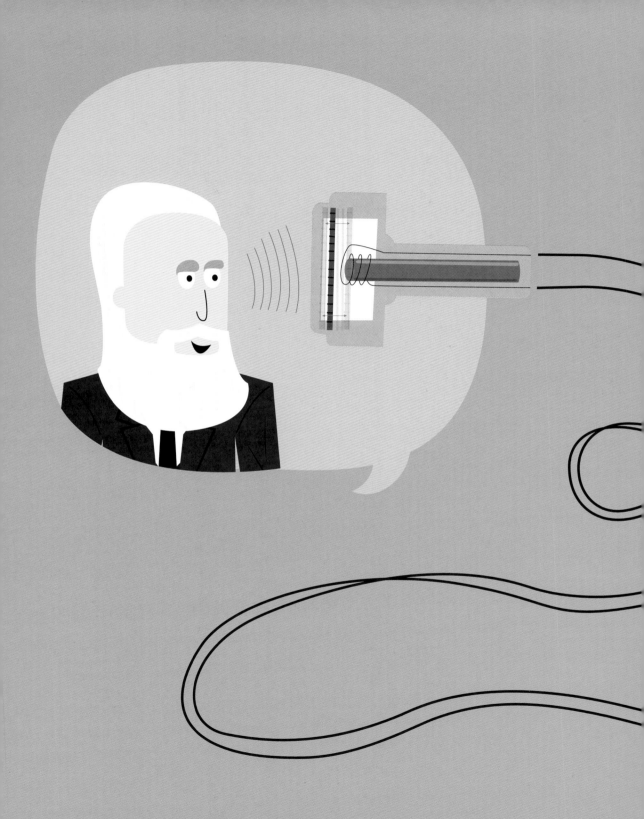

Communication

Humans love to communicate, but spoken words are limited—they don't travel far, however loudly you shout, and they don't last, either. The invention of writing was so important that people see it as the starting point of "history" itself. Once history was underway, it was filled with people inventing new ways to communicate—writing, printing, phoning, texting... Now we can communicate with people anywhere on the planet.

Communication Glossary

ARPANET Short for Advanced Research Projects Agency Network, the earliest version of the Internet.

Atlantic Ocean The ocean bordered by the Americas to the West and Europe and Africa to the East.

cuneiform The earliest known writing, used in Iraq 6,000 years ago, and made by pressing shapes into clay.

electromagnetic wave An energy wave that travels through space. Examples are light waves, radio waves, **X-rays**, and microwaves.

energy The power that makes other things happen. Electricity, radioactivity, heat, light, and sound are all kinds of energy.

engineer Somebody who uses scientific knowledge to make or design something to solve a practical problem.

hieroglyphic Picture-writing used in Ancient Egypt and some other early civilizations.

Internet The international network of computers.

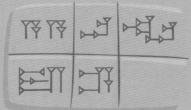

Internet Service Provider (ISP)
A company that offers access to the **Internet**.

patent A government license for an invention, it protects the inventor's idea.

radio transmitter A device that sends radio waves.

router A device that sends packets of data along computer networks, such as the **Internet**.

satellite An object that goes around the Earth, in space.

Solar System The Sun and the eight planets (including Earth) and smaller objects that orbit around it.

telegraph An early method of sending coded messages over long distances using electricity.

transducer A device that converts one form of energy to another. A microphone is the transducer that converts sound energy into electrical signals in a telephone.

X-ray A type of electromagnetic radiation that can travel through flesh and take a picture.

World Wide Web (WWW)
The system of rules and software that allows us to use the **Internet**.

Writing

... in 30 seconds

The handy thing about writing is that it records ideas—whether they are messages, poems, calculations, facts, or stories. Writing things down means that the ideas will last. Writing was one of our earliest inventions and it was well-established in Iraq by 4,000 BCE.

Writing began as a mixture of simple pictures of things (because they are easy to understand) and simple shapes such as lines and dots (because they are easy to make). To begin with, each written picture stood for a word. But this meant there were hundreds of different pictures to remember. In China, this system is still used, but in most other parts of the world, people began to use letters instead, with each letter standing for a different speech sound.

Over time, new inventions have changed the way we write. Paper was invented in China 2,000 years ago. Pencils and ballpoint pens have replaced sticks of charcoal and quill pens made from feathers. And now we do much of our writing not with a pen at all, but by tapping buttons on a keyboard or screen.

3-second sum-up

The invention of writing meant that ideas could be recorded.

3-minute mission Write hieroglyphics

You need: Computer, tablet, or smartphone • Paper and pens

Most Egyptian hieroglyphics are pictures. These pictures usually represent sounds, so a picture of an owl stands for the sound "m," for instance, and a lion for the sound "l." Write your name in hieroglyphics, using a website to help you find out which picture represents each letter. Try http://ngkids.co.uk/cool_stories/1036/hieroglyphics_uncovered.

Around the world, civilizations developed writing systems at different times.

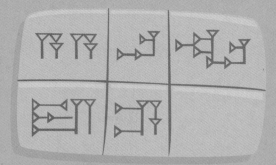

Cuneiform (c. 4,000 BCE)
The earliest writing.

Egyptian hieroglyphics (c. 3,000 BCE)
Each picture represents a word or sound.

Chinese writing (c. 1,100 BCE)
Usually written in columns.

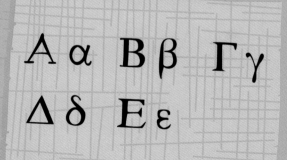

Ancient Greek (c. 800 BCE)
The source for all the modern scripts of Europe.

Mayan (c. 300 BCE)
Probably the most complex writing of all.

Printing press

... in 30 seconds

Until the 15th century, not many people in the Western world could read or write, partly because there wasn't much to read. Handwritten books did exist, but they were rare and expensive.

By 200 CE, some printing was taking place, but this took even longer than handwriting—a whole page of letters and illustrations had to be carved out of wood, before being covered in ink and printed on paper. But in 1439, an improved system was invented by Johann Gutenberg in Germany. Instead of carving out a whole page at a time, Gutenberg just carved out plenty of letters. He arranged these letter blocks on a wooden frame, spelling out a whole page before printing it. Since this process was so fast, books became more plentiful and less expensive.

Printing changed everything because knowledge could spread more rapidly and was no longer restricted to the rich. People were inspired to do many new things and had the information to help them. There were scientific breakthroughs, revolutions, changes in religions, new works of literature, more travel, and better education. The world would never be the same again.

3-second sum-up

The printing press spread knowledge to ordinary people and changed the world.

Most-printed books

1 *The Bible* (over 5 billion copies)
2 *The Qur'an* and *Quotations from the Works of Mao Tse-tung* (over 800 million copies each)
3 *Don Quixote* by Miguel de Cervantes (over 500 million copies)
4 *Xinhua* (Chinese) Dictionary (over 400 million copies)
5 *A Tale of Two Cities* by Charles Dickens (over 200 million copies)
6 *The Lord of the Rings* by J. R. R. Tolkien (over 150 million copies)

When books were written by hand, only the rich could afford them.

Gutenberg's printing press meant that books could be made cheaply and quickly, allowing ordinary people to read and learn.

Gutenberg's press used individual letter blocks, which could be rearranged easily and quickly to print new pages.

When the press was lowered, it squeezed the paper and inked letters together.

The letters were covered in ink and paper was placed on top.

THE BFG   Roald Dahl

The Lord of the Rings   J.R.R. Tolkein

ALICE'S ADVENTURES IN WONDERLAND   LEWIS CARROLL

THE LION, THE WITCH AND THE WARDROBE   C.S. Lewis

Treasure Island   Robert Louis Stevenson

HUCKLEBERRY FINN   MARK TWAIN

THE WIND IN THE WILLOWS   KENNETH GRAHAME

Charlotte's Web   E.B. White

OLIVER TWIST   Charles Dickens

Winnie the Pooh   A.A. Milne

GULLIVER'S TRAVELS   Jonathan Swift

ROBINSON CRUSOE   Daniel Defoe

The Jungle Book   Rudyard Kipling

FRANKENSTEIN   MARY SHELLEY

Black Beauty   Anna Sewell

PETER PAN   J.M. Barrie

Telephone

... in 30 seconds

There's one big name in telephone history: Alexander Graham Bell. In fact, the story of the phone involves many people having similar ideas at about the same time. But Bell was the one who got the patent in 1876, and therefore the fame.

Bell was inspired to invent the telephone while trying to improve the telegraph. The telegraph was one of the first communication devices to use electricity. It worked by sending pulses of electricity along a wire to be decoded at the other end. This meant that, for the first time, messages could be sent a very long way, very quickly. But the telegraph could only send signals, not voices.

Bell figured out how to send voices along wires by using transducers, which are devices that change energy from one form to another. At one end of the telephone, a transducer called a microphone turned sound into electricity. The electricity then traveled along a wire to another transducer (called a loudspeaker), where it was turned back into sound. For the first time people could communicate "live," with no need to wait for a reply.

3-second sum-up

Telephones carried voices through wires over vast distances.

3-minute mission Make a string telephone

You need: 2 disposable plastic cups • 65 ft (20 m) length of kite string or fishing line • An adult helper

Get an adult to pierce a hole in the middle of the base of each cup. Thread one end of the string through each hole and knot it. Get a friend to hold one cup to their ear and walk away until the string is taut. Speak into your cup, and your friend will hear what you say.

The string telephone works by changing sound waves to vibrations in a string, rather than to electrical patterns in a wire.

32

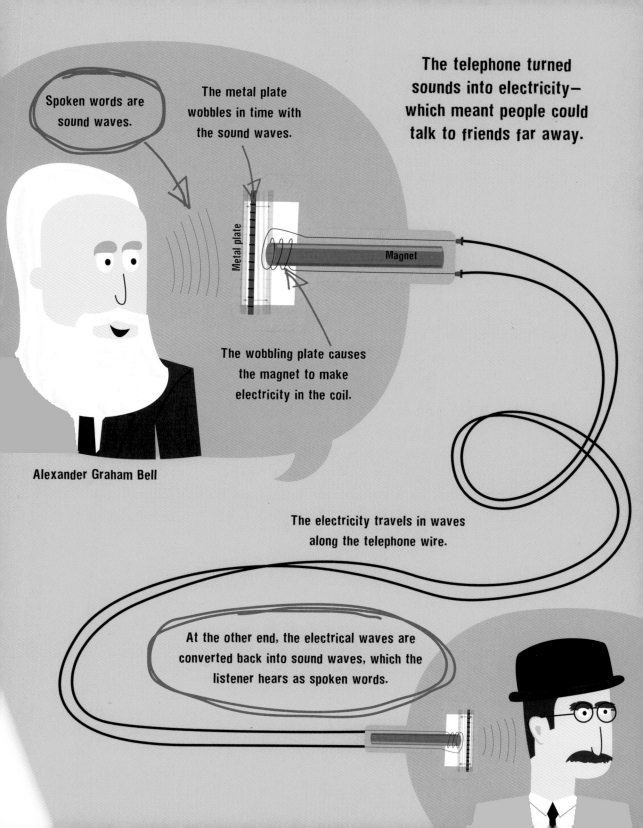

Radio

... in 30 seconds

The invention of the telephone was all very well, but all telephones needed one thing: wires. They were no good for ships at sea, nor for remote parts of the world. What was really needed were signals without wires—wireless communication.

In the 1860s, scientists started to study a newly discovered type of invisible wave—the radio wave. Like sound waves, radio waves move through air and solid objects—but they can travel much further than sound. In the 1890s, a young Italian inventor called Guglielmo Marconi succeeded in sending a radio signal across the Atlantic Ocean, and the age of radio began. Radio systems were built all over the world.

The earliest radios could only send beeps, so messages had to be coded, but soon voices and music could be sent, too. As a result, the radio broadcasting industry began. It became even more successful when people figured out how to convert light waves to radio waves, so that pictures could be sent by radio waves—what we now call television. Today, most phones also use radio waves, including all cell phones. It's a wireless world!

3-second sum-up

Radio allowed for communication between distant points on Earth—without wires.

3-minute mission Measure a microwave

Radio waves are one kind of electromagnetic wave. Light is another kind, and so are X-rays and microwaves. All these waves have different wavelengths (the distance between the peaks of the waves).

To measure the length of a microwave, heat a bar of unwrapped chocolate in a microwave oven for 15 seconds, removing the glass plate first. As the microwave passes through the bar, it melts the chocolate; the distance between the melted spots is half a microwave's wavelength.

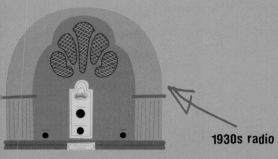

1930s radio

In 1907, inventors figured out how to send spoken words and music by radio waves.

Television was invented in the 1920s and used radio waves to send pictures.

Guglielmo Marconi

Since Marconi sent the very first radio signal in 1895, radio waves have been used for many different forms of communication.

All cell phones use radio waves.

Radio signals can even travel beyond the Solar System.

The Voyager 1 probe is 12 billion miles (20 billion kilometres) away and has been in radio contact since 1977.

Internet

... in 30 seconds

The latest and greatest invention in communications took most people by surprise—no one was expecting the Internet. In 1969, engineers linked together four US computers—each several miles from the others—by telephone lines, allowing them to exchange messages. This network was called ARPANET, and was the baby version of the Internet we know and love today.

The engineers' big problem was how to allow the computers to all talk at once, without the messages becoming jumbled. The solution was to break each computer's conversations into thousands of tiny chunks, called packets. As long as the packets specifically fitted into a message, they could be sent individually along different telephone lines and then be sorted out at the other end.

Today the Internet is a worldwide network of tens of millions of computers, and computer networks, all linked together by telephone wires and satellites. Thanks to the Internet, we can now chat with people anywhere on Earth—and see them at the same time. Information can flash across continents at lightning speed. We can buy and sell things anywhere, anytime, in seconds. And that's just the start...

3-second sum-up

The Internet is a worldwide network of computers that allows us to communicate instantly.

The World Wide Web

The Internet provides the vital links between computers all over the world, but using those links to view and use web pages relies on another invention, the World Wide Web (WWW), a kind of global computer program. While no single person invented the Internet, the World Wide Web was invented by Tim Berners Lee in 1989.

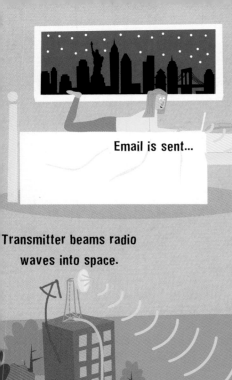

Email is sent...

SEND!

Thanks to the Internet, we can send messages instantly to friends on the other side of the world.

Radio waves go to router.

Router changes radio waves into electrical signals.

Transmitter beams radio waves into space.

Signals travel along telephone wire.

Signals reach Internet Service Provider (ISP), which sends signals to a radio transmitter.

Satellite receives radio signal and beams it out again across the world.

Signal received by another ISP.

RECEIVE!

Travel

There are many reasons to travel. Centuries ago, people were often on the move, searching for food, escaping enemies or building empires—or simply following a natural human desire to discover what was over the horizon. Now we travel to work, to learn, and to have fun. From the invention of the wheel to the latest high-tech spacecraft, new methods of travel have helped us explore the Earth and the Universe beyond.

Travel Glossary

Age of Sail The period from the 16th to the 19th century, when people traveled on large sailing ships to cross the seas for travel, trade, and war.

Atlantic Ocean The ocean bordered by the Americas to the West and Europe and Africa to the East.

axle The rod that connects the wheels in a vehicle.

boiler A water heater, often with pipes and a pump to send the heated water where it is needed.

carrack A very effective kind of sailing ship invented at the end of the 15th century.

cog A wheel with teeth, used to turn other cogs.

colonization Settling into and taking over a place.

combustion Burning.

crankshaft A long metal rod that connects a vehicle's engine to the wheels and turns them.

energy The power that makes other things happen. Electricity, radioactivity, heat, light, and sound are all kinds of energy.

engineer Somebody who uses scientific knowledge to make or design something to solve a practical problem.

Global Positioning System (GPS) A satellite-based navigation system that allows someone with a GPS device to know their exact location.

gravity The pull that holds you to the ground and keeps the Moon going around the Earth.

horseless carriage The early nickname for a car.

internal combustion engine An engine that burns the fuel inside itself, used in cars.

magnetic field The area around a magnet—and the Earth—where objects are pulled by it.

oxygen A gas in the air, needed for breathing and burning.

pneumatic Blown up with air.

poles The opposite ends of something, such as the Earth or a magnet.

portable Able to be carried or moved easily.

propeller A machine with rotating blades that propels (drives forward) a vehicle, such as a plane or a ship.

satellite An object that goes around the Earth, in space.

Slovenia A country in central Europe.

Space Age The period during which people explored space, beginning in 1957.

supersonic Faster than the speed of sound (770 miles per hour or 1,234 km per hour).

turbojet engine An engine used in airplanes that draws in air at the front and thrusts it out the back at high speed.

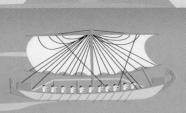

Wheel

... in 30 seconds

Wheels are all around us—it's impossible to imagine a world without them. We don't really know when or where the wheel was invented, but the earliest wheel that still exists was found in a swamp in Slovenia in 2002, along with its axle. It had lain there for more than 7,000 years.

How did the wheel come about? Well, moving an object that is too heavy to lift is tough. You can try dragging or shoving it, but a much easier method is to push it along on rollers—smooth, straight tree trunks were perfect for the job.

Gradually, over time, these early log rollers were adapted. First, they were cut away to make a thin rod (an axle) with a disc at either end (the wheels). These rollers had the advantage that they could be attached to a platform, which could be used to carry heavy objects. Later, the wheels and axle were made separately, which was much easier, and then joined together.

Once the wheel had been invented, people were able to travel much further and faster than before.

3-second sum-up

The invention of the wheel got things—and people—moving.

Cogs and gears

A new kind of wheel was invented in about 350 BCE, in Greece. Called a cog or gear, this wheel had teeth, which interlocked with the teeth on another wheel and made it turn. That wasn't all— if the second wheel was smaller than the first, with half as many teeth, it would turn twice as fast. This meant that machines could be made that contained wheels that turned at different speeds— such as a clock, with its hour and minute hands.

Before the wheel, people used rollers to move things around.

As the wheel developed, travel got smoother and moving loads became easier.

Rollers attached to a platform became the first carts.

Attaching wheels to a separate axle was the next step.

Spokes were invented 4,000 years ago.

Pneumatic (air-filled) tires, invented in 1845, meant a less bumpy ride.

Wheels became light and flexible.

Today's wheels are strong and grip the road.

Compass

... in 30 seconds

Thousands of years ago, people had no idea where they were on the planet (in fact, they didn't even know they lived on one). Travelers made use of the Sun—which rises in the east and sets in the west—to keep track of the direction they were going.

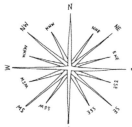

Then, about 2,000 years ago, an unknown Chinese person invented an amazing device—the compass. Simply a spoon-shaped piece of metal sitting on a plate, it always pointed north. How did it work? A compass is a magnet, and if it is free to move, it will spin so that one of its ends points to a nearby magnet. By an enormous piece of good luck, our planet has a magnet inside and the ends of this magnet are roughly at the North Pole and South Pole of the Earth. This means that one end of a compass will always turn to point north.

Over time, the spoon-shaped compass was replaced by a magnetic needle floating in water, and then by a needle mounted on a pin. This compass was simpler to carry and allowed people to explore and map the Earth much more easily than ever before.

3-second sum-up

A compass is a magnet that shows you where you're headed by pointing to the Earth's poles.

3-minute mission Make a compass

You need: A needle • A bar magnet • A small dish • A smaller lid

Stroke a needle with one end of the magnet 50 times. (Stroke in the same direction each time.) Half-fill the dish with water and float the lid in it. Place the needle on the lid. The lid and needle will turn slowly to point north.

A compass needle uses the Earth's magnetism to always point north. For centuries travelers have used it to help them find their way.

The earliest compasses were Chinese, and were used for fortune-telling, not navigating.

Geographical North Pole/ magnetic South Pole

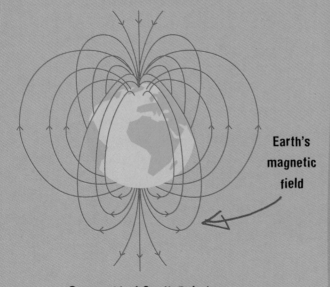

Earth's magnetic field

Geographical South Pole/ magnetic North Pole

In the 14th century, portable compasses allowed people to explore the world.

This modern compass locates north by using the satellites of the Global Positioning System (GPS).

Sailing ship

... in 30 seconds

For early humans, the sea was a dangerous place, but a useful source of food. By floating on simple boats, people could catch many fish, and travel along the coast to explore, too. But to cross the seas to other lands, something safer, bigger, and faster was needed—a sailing ship, pushed along by the wind.

The first sailing ships were made thousands of years ago in Egypt, but the great Age of Sail really began with the carrack, developed in the 15th and 16th centuries by several countries in western Europe. The carrack performed so much better than any other boat on the seas that many sailing ships like it were soon traveling every ocean and sea on Earth. The famous explorer Christopher Columbus voyaged around the world in the 1490s in a carrack called *Santa Maria*.

Exploration was only the start of the story. Depending on what the sailors found on the shores they reached, sailing led to colonization, trade, conquest, or war. One way or another, the countries of the world were now in touch.

3-second sum-up

Sailing ships made travel between distant countries possible.

Designing the carrack

The design of the carrack was driven by the need for much sturdier, ocean-going ships. In 15th-century western Europe, exploration and trade was expanding, and carracks could be used to travel the world. Instead of two masts, carracks had three or four, and a new type of rigging that made them able to handle the strong winds far out at sea. They were also big enough to be stable in stormy seas and had plenty of space for supplies, making them ideal for longer voyages.

Steam train

... in 30 seconds

The world we live in today is very different from that of the 17th century. That is mainly thanks to one invention—the steam engine, which captured the energy of burning fuel (usually coal) and turned it into motion.

Early steam engines were heavy and not very powerful, but in the 1870s several US engineers started to build some light enough to power vehicles. In Wales in 1804, an experimental steam locomotive designed by Richard Trevithick trundled along a short stretch of iron rails. In 1829 a really good locomotive, called *Rocket*, was built in England by George Stephenson. Stephenson also laid the first proper railway in the world, between Stockton and Darlington in the UK.

In the 1830s there was a frenzy of track-laying in Europe, North America, and Australia. Now, factories and farms could sell their goods to places a long way away, and people could travel far and fast, for work and pleasure. Although steam trains are long gone, electrical and diesel-powered trains are still vital to trade and travel today.

3-second sum-up

Steam trains used the power of the steam engine to get people and goods moving.

Powered by steam

1769 The first steam cars are built, but they never really catch on.

1893 George Moore builds a steam-powered robot and goes for walks with it in New York City.

1897 The first of many steam-turbine-powered ships are built.

1933 The first, and only, steam-powered plane takes to the air.

2001 A new kind of rocket thruster is designed, using steam power to push tiny satellites through space.

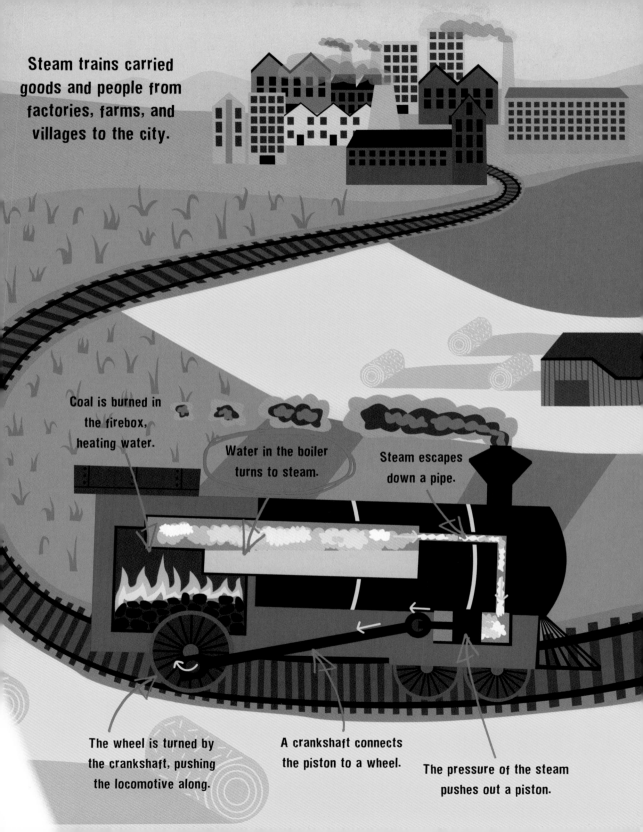

Steam trains carried goods and people from factories, farms, and villages to the city.

Coal is burned in the firebox, heating water.

Water in the boiler turns to steam.

Steam escapes down a pipe.

The wheel is turned by the crankshaft, pushing the locomotive along.

A crankshaft connects the piston to a wheel.

The pressure of the steam pushes out a piston.

Car

... in 30 seconds

Steam trains were very popular, but they didn't always take people exactly where they needed to go. What was really needed was an invention to replace horse-drawn carts and carriages—in other words, a horseless carriage, or "car" for short.

The question was how to power cars. Steam engines just weren't suitable—even the smallest was much too big, and they took a long time to get going. Luckily, Claude and Nicéphore Niépce had already made a breakthrough invention in 1807—the "internal combustion engine." Rather than the fire ("combustion") taking place outside the boiler as in a steam engine, this new engine kept the combustion inside. After decades of improvement by inventors, this engine was used in the first successful car, the Benz Patent Motor Car, in 1879.

For the first few decades, cars were very expensive. Since then, they have become faster and cheaper, and are better designed. Now, a new kind of car is beginning to be made in large numbers: an electric one.

3-second sum-up

Unlike trains, cars can take people wherever they want to go, whenever they want to go.

Record-breaking cars

Longest car: The Cadillac limousine is 100 ft (30.5 m) long, with 26 wheels. Three of these limousines, end-to-end, are the length of a soccer field.

Fastest mass-produced car: The Bugatti Veyron Super Sport can reach 268 miles per hour (431 km per hour)—more than three times faster than the top speed on a highway.

Fastest specially built car: The ThrustSSC (1997) holds the Land Speed Record. It reached 763 miles per hour (1,228 km per hour)—faster than the speed of sound.

The internal combustion engine was the solution to powering the car.

In an internal combustion engine, fuel is exploded inside one of several cylinders, moving a piston that pushes the wheels around.

1. INTAKE

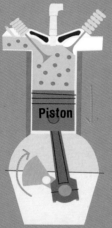

Air and fuel are sucked into the cylinder as piston moves down.

2. COMPRESSION

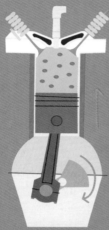

As the piston rises, the air and fuel are squeezed hard.

3. POWER

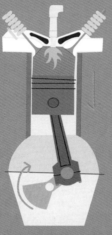

A spark makes the fuel explode, forcing the piston down.

4. EXHAUST

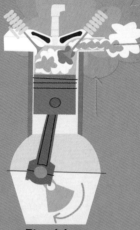

The rising piston forces out the leftovers (exhaust) from the explosion.

Today's hybrid cars have an electric motor as well as an internal combustion engine.

Benz's Motorwagen (1885)

Ford's Model T (1908)

Modern hybrid car

Airplane

... in 30 seconds

People have been trying to fly for centuries, and for most of those centuries they got nowhere but down. The main problem was that inventors tried to copy birds, with flapping wings. But human muscle just isn't strong enough to power bird-like wings, and making a flapping-wing machine is extremely hard.

The first humans to take to the air used hot-air balloons and simple gliders, but both of these flying machines tend to go where the wind, rather than the pilot, directs. What the world needed was a powered flying machine. In 1903, Orville Wright launched himself into the air on the first one, with the help of his brother Wilbur. The flight was short but the air was conquered. Within decades, airplanes swept across the world's skies.

All of these early airplanes were driven by propellers, that limited their speed, but in 1930 an engineer named Fred Whipple invented the turbojet engine. In 1947, a jet plane went supersonic (faster than the speed of sound) for the first time. All of today's large planes are powered by jet engines.

3-second sum-up

Planes take people over any kind of land or water—fast.

3-minute mission Shaped for speed

The shape of an aircraft's wings affects how fast it can fly. Using two identical pieces of rectangular paper, make two paper airplanes, one wide, one narrow (start one from the short side and one from the long side). See which flies faster. Try making even narrower paper airplanes—is there a limit to how fast you can make them fly?

Over the centuries, aircraft have flown further and faster.

**Montgolfier brothers
(France, 1783)
First crewed
hot-air balloon**

**Wright Flyer 1
(USA, 1903)
First powered flying machine**

Propellers push the
plane forward.

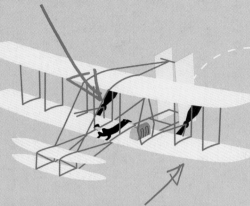

Tilted wings push air downward and
wings upward, lifting the plane up.

**Heinkel He 178
(Germany, 1939)
First jet plane**

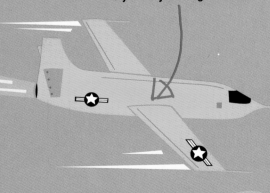

**Bell X-1
(USA, 1947)
First supersonic plane**

Powerful engines and a
"streamlined" body allow the plane
to fly easily through the air.

A burning jet of gas draws in
air at the front of the engine
and pushes it out at the back,
thrusting the plane forward.

Spacecraft

... in 30 seconds

People have a natural urge to explore, and once we had been everywhere on Earth, the only place left to explore was space. But how to get there? Planes are no use—they need air to fly, but there is no air in space. The only way to get to space is by rocket.

In 1926, a US engineer named Robert Goddard invented a rocket that worked by burning liquid fuel and using its own oxygen supply. Goddard's invention was the beginning of the Space Age. From then on, rockets—and the spacecraft they launched into space— developed steadily.

The first piloted spacecraft was the USSR's Vostok 1, which carried Yuri Gagarin on an orbit around the Earth in 1961. Eight years later an enormous rocket-powered spacecraft, Apollo 11, landed three astronauts on the Moon. Since then, spacecraft have explored all the planets and many of the moons of the Solar System, taken crews to space stations and even taken tourists for vacations in orbit. Although several different methods (including gravity, electricity, and sunlight) have been used to steer spacecraft through space, rockets are the only way to get them there.

3-second sum-up

Spacecraft have landed people on the Moon—and may take us anywhere, given time.

3-minute mission:
Make a balloon-powered rocket

You need: 26 ft (8 m) of fishing line • A straw • A long balloon • Adhesive tape • An adult helper

Pass the line through the straw and tie the ends to trees 20 ft (6 m) apart, so that the line is taut. Inflate the balloon, hold it closed, and tape it to the straw so that it is lined up with the string. Pull the balloon to one end of the line, and let go!

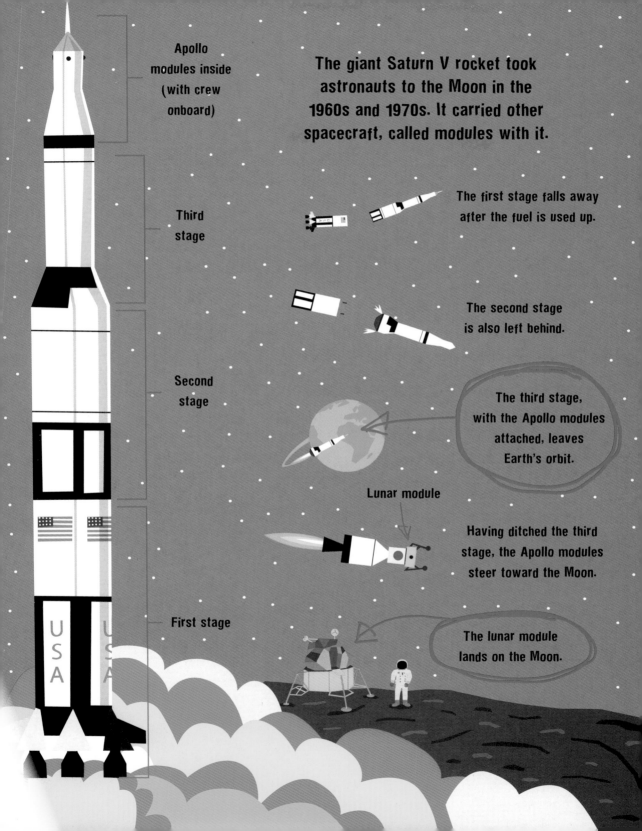

Apollo
modules inside
(with crew
onboard)

Third
stage

Second
stage

First stage

The giant Saturn V rocket took
astronauts to the Moon in the
1960s and 1970s. It carried other
spacecraft, called modules with it.

The first stage falls away
after the fuel is used up.

The second stage
is also left behind.

The third stage,
with the Apollo modules
attached, leaves
Earth's orbit.

Lunar module

Having ditched the third
stage, the Apollo modules
steer toward the Moon.

The lunar module
lands on the Moon.

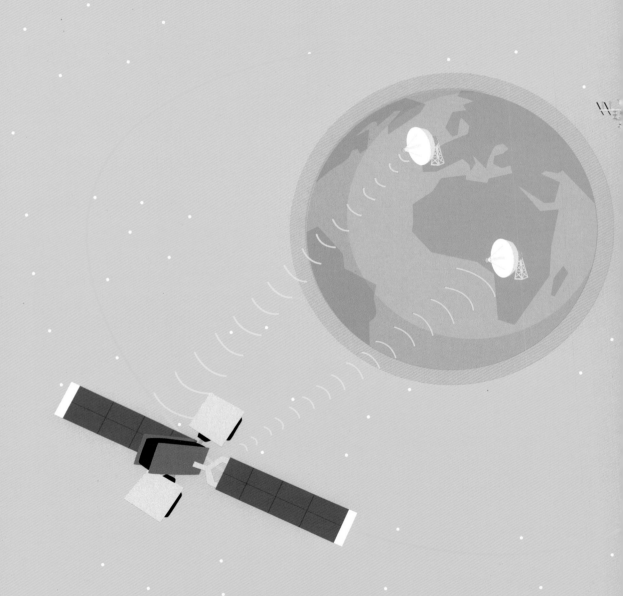

Finding out

We have been trying to understand the world for thousands of years, and many inventions have helped us in our quest for knowledge. Today, we can peer inside living things, watch our own planet from orbiting satellites, gaze at stars trillions of miles away—and use immensely powerful computers to make sense of it all.

Finding out
Glossary

atom A tiny particle, from which everything we see around us is made. Atoms contain even smaller particles, including neutrons and electrons.

cog A wheel with teeth, used to turn other cogs.

computer Device that can be given instructions to carry out many different calculations.

Global Positioning System (GPS) A satellite-based navigation system that allows someone with a GPS device to know their exact location.

gravity The pull that holds you to the ground and keeps the Moon going around the Earth.

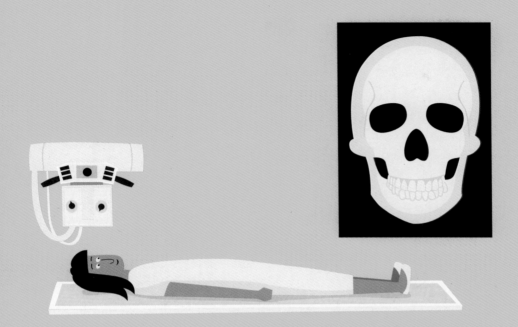

Internet The international network of computers.

lens A shaped piece of glass or plastic that bends light.

poles The opposite ends of something, such as the Earth or a magnet.

refraction The bending or deflection of light or other waves.

satellite An object that goes around the Earth, in space.

trillion A million million.

Universe Everything that exists.

vowel In English, the letters a, e, i, o and u. Nearly all words contain vowels.

X-ray A type of electromagnetic radiation that can travel through flesh.

Telescope
... in 30 seconds

We know a great deal about the Universe, including where it came from, how big it is and where the Earth fits in it. The tool that has taught us all this is the telescope, an instrument that makes things look both closer and brighter.

The telescope was invented by a German glasses maker, Hans Lipperhey, in 1608. The following year, the Italian scientist Galileo Galilei built an improved version. Over a few nights he discovered more things in outer space than had been found in the previous 10,000 years. Telescopes have been improving ever since. Some are so powerful that they can see more than halfway across our Universe—many trillions of trillions of miles.

The secret of the telescope is a shaped piece of clear material, such as glass, called a lens, which changes the directions of light rays that pass through it. Galileo's telescope used two lenses: a big one to collect the light and a small one to focus it on the eye. In 1671, Isaac Newton swapped the big lens for a curved mirror, and all big telescopes are now based on this design.

3-second sum-up

Telescopes magnify things far away and show us new worlds.

3-minute mission Make a telescope

You need: 1 small and 1 large magnifying glass

Choose a clear object such as a streetlight at night or a tree on the horizon in daytime. Hold the small magnifying glass close to one eye (close the other eye if you like). Hold the large magnifying glass close to the small one and gradually move it away, looking through both lenses at your object, until it is sharp and clear.

Never look directly at the Sun!

Two main types of telescopes are used to explore the night skies.

Refracting telescopes use two lenses.

Reflecting telescopes use a lens and mirrors.

Large lens captures lots of light and bends it toward a focal point, where the light rays cross.

Large curved mirror captures lots of light and reflects it toward a focal point.

Small "eyepiece" lens forms a sharp image.

A second mirror reflects light toward the side of the telescope.

"Eyepiece" lens forms a sharp image.

X-rays

... in 30 seconds

X-rays were discovered by accident in 1895 by a German scientist named William Röntgen. He was experimenting with electricity by passing it through a tube, when he noticed a strange glow coming from a screen nearby. The glow came and went when he switched the electricity on and off, so he decided that invisible rays—which he named "X-rays"—must be traveling from the tube to the screen.

When Röntgen experimented with the rays, he found that they could pass easily through some materials, such as flesh, which light cannot. But they could not pass through bone, and this led to a breakthrough. If you place a person between an X-ray source and a photographic plate, their bones will stop the rays—and create an X-ray photograph. The very first X-ray photograph was of Röntgen's wife's hand—"I have seen my death," she groaned, horrified.

X-rays have been revealing the insides of people ever since, helping to save many lives. They are now used for much more besides, including astronomy and investigating the structure of groups of atoms.

3-second sum-up

X-rays are invisible rays that allow us to see inside ourselves.

3-minute mission Look inside yourself

Get a bright flashlight—one with as wide a light end as possible. In a dark room, place your hand over the light end and switch it on. Just like X-rays, the bright light will pass through your flesh but not your bones, so you will see more or less what Mrs. Röntgen did.

The discovery of X-rays has changed the way we understand our bodies and our world.

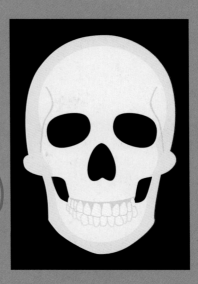

X-ray machines allow doctors to see what's underneath the skin without cutting the patient open.

The Chandra X-ray telescope orbits the Earth and detects X-rays produced in long-ago star explosions.

X-rays enter here

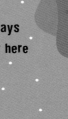

Solar panels

X-ray camera

Computer

... in 30 seconds

Charles Babbage was a brilliant but impatient man, and one of the things he was impatient about was the many errors that turned up in mathematical tables. These tables were needed for all sorts of things, from bridge building to banking. Since the mistakes were caused by people, in 1812 Babbage decided to build a machine to calculate and print the tables instead.

Before the machine (called a Difference Engine) was built, Babbage had an even more brilliant idea. Rather than building a machine to work out a mathematical table, why not invent one that could be programmed to work out ANYTHING? Babbage called this an Analytical Engine—and we call it a computer. Sadly, Babbage didn't get very far with building his machine, partly because, being mechanical, it needed huge numbers of precisely made cogs.

Once people had invented new kinds of electrical devices, they tried again to build computers. The first computers were made in the 1940s and used only for calculations, but today they deal with information of all kinds and are EVERYWHERE—in your TV, your cell phone, your camera, and your MP3 player.

3-second sum-up

Computers handle information faster and better than we do.

3-minute mission Information squeeze

The job of every computer is handling information, often vast amounts of it. To save space and time, they usually "compress" information so that it still makes sense but takes up less space.

Try it yourself: write a long sentence out in full and then write it again without the vowels. Does it still make sense? To find out, see if a friend can understand it.

The first electronic computers were huge and unreliable, but soon much smaller and better ones were being built —and they keep on getting smaller and more powerful.

Charles Babbage's Analytical Engine—the first computer— was mechanical, and used cogs to work out calculations.

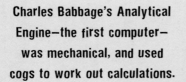

The first electronic computers, such as the 1940s military computer ENIAC, were vast. ENIAC took up several rooms, and used more than 23,000 electronic parts to make its calculations.

The "brain" or central processing unit, in today's enormously powerful computers is built entirely into a single tiny microchip the size of a bee.

Satellite

... in 30 seconds

A satellite is an object that travels through space around the Earth. The Moon is a natural satellite of the Earth, but there are artificial ones too, placed into orbit by spacecraft. The very first one was Sputnik 1, launched by the USSR in 1957, partly to show its US rivals how advanced Soviet technology was. Soon, many more satellites were launched by both countries.

Once a satellite is in space, it orbits steadily, with no need for power to keep going. The further out it is from Earth, the slower it moves.

Satellites communicate with Earth by sending and receiving radio signals, and they perform many jobs. Some are orbiting telescopes, with views of the Universe far clearer than any from Earth. Other satellites watch the weather, tell people where they are (a system called the Global Positioning System, or GPS), spy on other countries or bounce phone calls, Internet data and TV programs from one continent to another. Some satellites even have people on board; these are called space stations.

3-second sum-up

Satellites orbit the Earth, keeping people in touch, doing research, spying, and more.

3-minute mission Satellite speed

Take a large, light, plastic plate. Add a tennis ball. Move the plate until the ball rolls smoothly around the edge. What happens if you go too fast or slow?

Satellites work just like this. To orbit, they must have just the right speed. Too slow and the Earth's gravity pulls them down (just like it pulls the ball to the center of the plate). Too fast and they will break free of their orbits and hurtle off into outer space.

Satellites orbit around
the Earth and do many
different jobs.

Moon

The International Space Station is
a research laboratory run by astronauts
from many different countries.

The French SPOT satellite
monitors the Earth's climate.

The Intelsat 28 satellite
beams TV and Internet signals
from one country to another,
using radio waves.

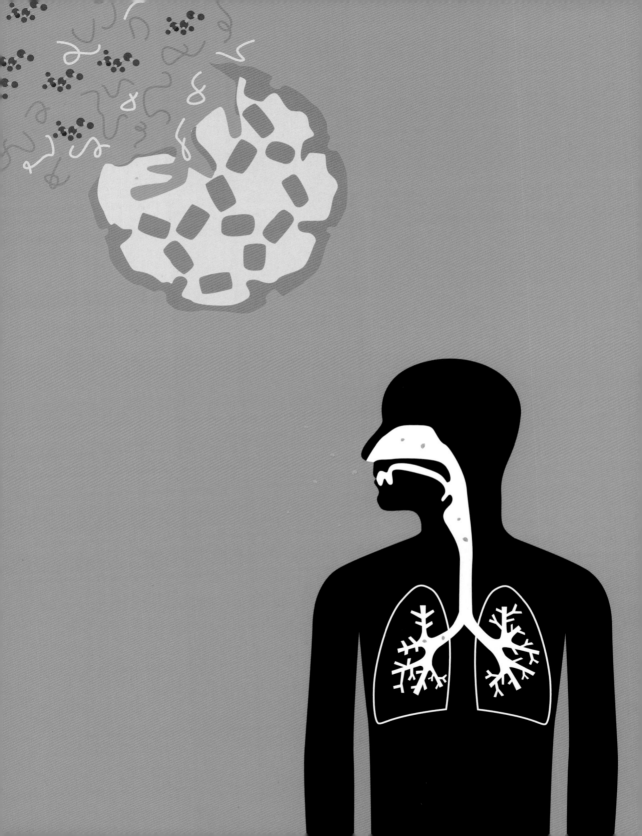

Medicine

It's no surprise that medical treatments have always been high on the list of "inventions wanted". As in other areas of invention, the earliest breakthroughs involved using natural products found to have useful properties. But as people learned more about science, they were able to devise tailor-made cures and treatments, so that today's doctors can treat almost anything.

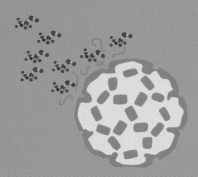

Medicine Glossary

anesthetic A chemical used in operations to prevent the patient from feeling pain.

antibiotic A medicine (such as penicillin) that kills bacteria inside the body.

antiseptic A chemical that kills germs.

bacterium (plural bacteria) A tiny living thing, too small to see, which may cause an illness. Bacteria are a kind of germ.

general anesthetic A strong painkiller that puts a person to sleep.

germ A tiny living thing or a complicated chemical, too small to see without a microscope, that causes diseases.

immune No longer able to catch a particular disease.

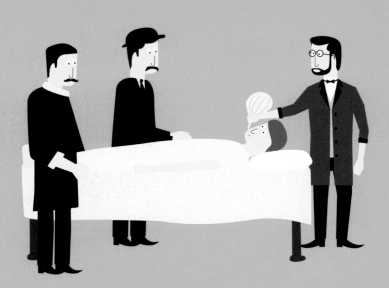

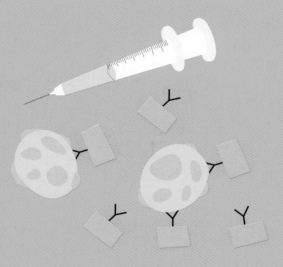

implant Something that replaces a part of the body.

pacemaker Some people's hearts cannot beat properly on their own. A pacemaker is a device that helps these hearts to beat.

prosthesis An implant that replaces an outside part of the body, such as an arm, leg, or nose.

smallpox A dangerous disease that killed many millions of people in the past.

vaccine A type of medicine that helps prevent a particular disease from being caught in future.

virus A chemical so complicated it is almost alive. Viruses are **germs**, and some viruses can cause illness.

Vaccination

... in 30 seconds

Edward Jenner was an 18th-century country doctor who, like all other doctors at the time, was faced with a stream of patients for whom he could do nothing. They had smallpox, a disease that killed many and left most survivors with horribly scarred faces.

In the 1760s, Jenner decided to investigate a strange rumor: milkmaids were said never to catch smallpox. Suppose, he thought, this were true? Jenner knew that milkmaids commonly suffered from a related disease called cowpox, which they caught from the cows. Though unpleasant, it was not fatal. Could that be the answer?

Jenner tried a dangerous experiment. He infected a healthy boy first with pus from the blisters of a milkmaid with cowpox, and then with the smallpox virus—and found that the boy did not develop the deadly disease. He had become "immune" to it. Jenner's success saved millions of lives, and we still use versions of this approach today.

3-second sum-up

Vaccines teach your body to fight infections.

Killer diseases

Vaccination has saved countless lives since its invention. A vaccine for rabies, a deadly disease spread by animal bites, was created in 1885, using the nerves from rabid rabbits. The same year saw a vaccine for cholera, a disease that had killed tens of millions of people earlier that century. A typhoid vaccine arrived in 1896, and was used by troops in World War I. And two centuries after Jenner's discovery, smallpox was eventually wiped out across the world, thanks to vaccination.

Vaccinations protect against many diseases, from measles to flu.

When the flu vaccine is injected, it circulates weak virus particles, called antigens, in the blood.

The body produces immune cells, which attach themselves to the antigens.

Immune cells

Antigens

When a full-strength flu virus is breathed in, the immune cells are ready.

The immune cells recognize the flu virus and kill it.

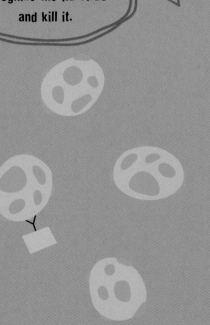

Painkillers

... in 30 seconds

A few hundred years ago, medical operations were little better than torture. If you had an infected leg, you'd be held down while a surgeon sawed it off and then dipped the stump in hot tar.

Then, in 1799, an inventor called Humphry Davy had a breakthrough. He discovered that a gas called nitrous oxide had strange effects on people—it made them giggly and also reduced the pain they felt. Later, other chemicals were found that did an even better job. Some even put people into a deep, pain-free sleep.

All these pain-killing chemicals didn't just make medical operations bearable for the patients—a calm or sleeping patient can be operated on for longer and more carefully, so all sorts of new operations became possible.

Once aspirin had been invented in 1897, common complaints such as headaches could be treated, too. Now, pain control is a major part of medicine, and almost any pain can be reduced or removed.

3-second sum-up

Painkillers mean surgery without agony.

Surgery before painkillers

Before the 19th century, people would only have an operation if they had no other choice. There were no painkillers, just a stick of wood to bite down on, and your chances of survival weren't that great either. In some London hospitals, 8 out of 10 patients died after an operation—some from blood loss or infection, and some just from the shock. No wonder that most people simply refused to have surgery.

Once anesthetics had been invented, operations became less painful and much safer.

Before painkillers, surgeons only operated as a last resort.

Laughing gas was one of the first "anesthetics"—substances that work by preventing nerves from sending pain signals to the brain.

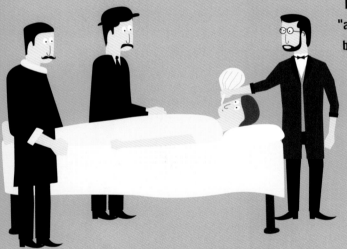

General anesthetics put people into a deep sleep, and were a big step forward for major operations.

Germ killers

... in 30 seconds

It was only in the 19th century that scientists—especially the great Louis Pasteur—finally proved that diseases are caused by "germs" too small to see without a microscope. Some germs are tiny living things called bacteria, while others are complicated chemicals called viruses.

Once disease germs had been discovered, it wasn't long before ways to kill them were found. Just heating milk, for instance, is enough to make it germ-free. A tougher challenge was how to kill the germs on or in people.

Germs killed so many people after surgery that operations were rarely carried out. The problem was solved by Joseph Lister in 1867, when he discovered that phenol (carbolic acid) was an "antiseptic"—a chemical that killed germs on the skin or on surgical instruments.

The most important germ killer of all was discovered in 1928 by Alexander Fleming—by complete accident. Called penicillin, it is made from the mold found on blue cheese, and it was the first antibiotic, which is a substance that can kill bacteria inside the body. Penicillin saved millions of lives and is still used today.

3-second sum-up

Antiseptics and antibiotics kill germs and save lives.

3-minute mission Grow mold

You need: Bouillon cubes • 2 transparent cups • Plastic wrap • An adult helper

Prepare some soup stock and half-fill two cups with it. Re-boil one cup in a microwave, allow it to cool and cover it with plastic wrap. Leave the other cup open. Put both cups in a warm place. Within a week or so, mold will appear on one but not the other. The heat killed all the germs in both cups, but dust brought new germs to the open bowl, while the sealed bowl remained germ-free.

Antibiotics kill germs within the body.

Antibiotic pills

Penicillin (a type of antibiotic) kills bacteria by making its skin split. The inside of the bacterium oozes out and dies, leaving a corpse called a "spheroplast."

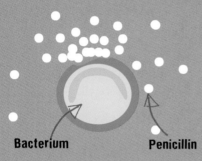

Bacterium

Penicillin

Spheroplast

Antiseptics kill germs on the body.

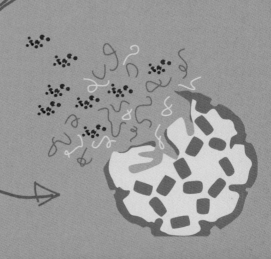

Antiseptic liquid is wiped on cuts and abrasions to kill germs before they can get inside the body.

Ethanol (a type of antiseptic) kills virus particles by unwinding the long, coiled strands they are made of, so that they fall apart.

Ethanol

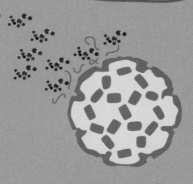

Virus particle

Implants

... in 30 seconds

Your body is like a machine made of many smaller machines. The heart is a blood-pump, the eyes are cameras and the muscles are motors. When a machine goes wrong, or wears out, or is damaged, its parts can be replaced—and so can those of the body.

Machines that replace a part of the body are called implants. When an implant replaces a leg or hand, the new part is called a prosthesis. Simple prostheses such as peg-legs and hook-hands have been used for thousands of years, but today's prostheses can look very real. "Myoelectric" devices, invented in 1964, can even be controlled just like the real things—by the brain.

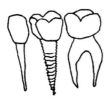

One of the first implants to be put inside a body was a pacemaker, invented in 1932. Since then, many other implants have been invented, including artificial teeth, hearing devices, and vision systems. In the last few years, scientists have started to grow implants from living flesh. If they succeed, there may one day be no part of the body that cannot be replaced.

3-second sum-up

Many parts of the body can be replaced by machines.

3-minute mission
Design your own super-implant

In the future, implants might be used to improve on natural bodies, making longer-lasting hearts, lungs that filter out pollution, or stronger muscles—even extra memory or seeing heat-rays might be possible. What super-implant would you choose? Design your own, then draw and label your invention.

Implants replace parts of the body that do not work or have been damaged or worn-out.

A cochlear (inner ear) implant picks up signals from a microphone, helping deaf people to hear.

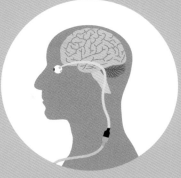

An implant fixed inside the eye sends electrical signals to the brain, giving blind people some sight.

Brain-controlled robotic arms use motors instead of muscles.

A metal ball and socket replaces worn-out hip joints. Implants inside the body are made from material the body won't reject.

Pacemakers send jolts of electricity to the heart to control how fast it beats.

Industry

In a way, the world we live in is a huge
and complicated invention, full of systems to
grow food, make and sell goods, build houses,
generate power, and more. All these systems
are industries, and industries are based on
some key inventions.

Industry Glossary

actuator A device that moves the arm or other part of a robot.

atom A tiny particle, from which everything we see around us is made. Atoms contain even smaller particles, including neutrons and electrons.

boiler A water heater, often with pipes and a pump to send the heated water where it is needed.

computer Device that can be given instructions to carry out many different calculations.

disintegrate To fall apart. The atoms of radioactive elements disintegrate.

electronic Devices that work thanks to the behavior of tiny units of electricity called electrons.

elements A substance that cannot be divided into simpler substances. There are about 100 elements, from which all other substances are made. Oxygen and radium are elements.

energy The power that makes other things happen. Electricity, radioactivity, heat, light, and sound are all kinds of energy.

fission Splitting into two or more parts.

generator A machine that turns mechanical energy (such as that created by a turbine) into electricity.

laser A device that makes a light beam of an exact color that is very focused and can carry a great deal of energy.

neutron A particle that usually forms part of an **atom** but which can be set free and used to break other atoms apart.

nuclear Having to do with the cores, or nuclei, of **atoms**.

nuclear reactor An invention that uses nuclear fuel to produce electrical power.

radioactive Producing dangerous rays and particles.

radium Radioactive element that glows in the dark and never cools down.

robot A machine that can be programmed to perform complicated tasks usually done by people.

ruby A precious red jewel, used in the first lasers.

transistor A device that controls the direction or size of a flow of electricity.

turbine An invention containing a wheel that is spun by wind, water, or steam, which then turns something else.

uranium A radioactive element used as fuel in nuclear reactors.

wi-fi A wireless technology that allows electronic devices to connect to each other or the Internet using radio waves instead of wires.

Transistor

... in 30 seconds

Most of today's gadgets—including TVs, computers, and MP3 players—use electricity to control what they do. Such gadgets are referred to as "electronic", and the building blocks of all electronic devices are transistors.

Transistors work very much like a tap controlling the flow of water. Depending on what you do with it, it can start, increase or stop the flow of electricity through a wire. The first transistor, invented in 1947, was several inches high, but today's transistors are much too small to see without a microscope, and millions are packed into every electronic device.

Some people say that the transistor was the greatest 20th-century invention. Transistors were smaller, sturdier, longer-lasting, faster, cheaper, and less power-hungry than the vacuum-tube technology they replaced. So electronic devices became smaller, cheaper, tougher, and faster, too. Without the transistor, our cars, washing machines, and computers would be massive and unreliable, and compact devices such as cell phones and laptops would not even exist.

3-second sum-up

Transistors make gadgets smaller, faster, cheaper, and better.

Rock 'n' roll radios

The radio was transformed by the transistor. Old radios were expensive, large and heavy—and stayed in one place. Transistorized radios, introduced in 1954, were cheap, small, and battery-powered, which meant that people could listen to what they wanted, where they wanted, whenever they liked. And all thanks to the transistor. No wonder these revolutionary new radios were simply called "transistors."

Helicopter

Transistors are all around us, not just in computers but in everything electronic, from elevators to helicopters.

TVs and radios were the first transistorized devices used in the home.

Elevator

TVs

Motorcycle

Camera

Car

Laptop

MP3 player

Computers are now smaller, cheaper, and more powerful, thanks to transistors.

Every year transistors get smaller and smaller. Even a tiny MP3 player contains millions of transistors.

Nuclear reactor

... in 30 seconds

In 1902, Marie and Pierre Curie succeeded in extracting a strange new chemical from a mysterious black mineral called pitchblende. The chemical glowed in the dark and gave out heat constantly. It did this because one of its components was radium, which is a radioactive element—that is, it gives off radiation.

Radioactive atoms produce heat by splitting, or "disintegrating." Each disintegration releases neutrons—tiny bullet-like particles— that set off several more disintegrations, producing a chain reaction of heat. Designing nuclear reactors is all about controlling these neutrons to get the right amount of heat.

Scientist Leó Szilárd helped build the world's first experimental nuclear reactor in 1942 at the University of Chicago, using the radioactive element uranium. The invention was a success, and during the 1950s nuclear reactors were built in several countries. The power they release is enormous: a single gram of Uranium 235 produces as much energy as 3 tonnes of coal. Today's reactors supply more than 11 percent of the world's electricity.

3-second sum-up

Nuclear reactors use the energy locked inside atoms to make electricity.

3-minute mission Build a nuclear reactor

You need: 10 tennis balls • 9 toilet paper tubes

Stand the tubes in a cluster, with one ball balanced on each. Then roll the other ball at them. The balls are like neutrons— once released, they release more neutrons. Can you make all the balls fall together (like a nuclear bomb) or one after the other (like a nuclear reactor)? As you'll see, bombs are easier to build than reactors!

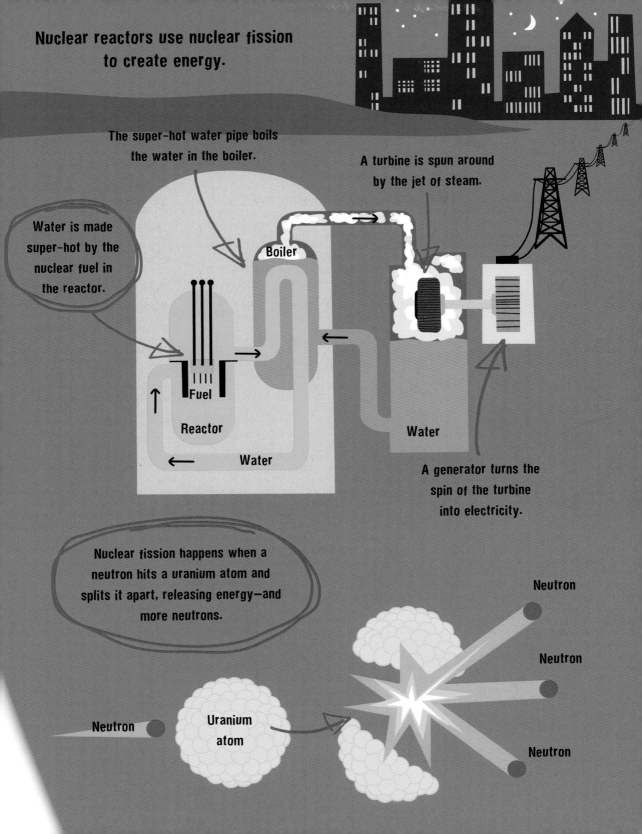

Laser

... in 30 seconds

A laser makes a very special kind of light, of exactly one color, in a beam that hardly spreads out at all and so can be focused on one tiny spot, making it very powerful. Albert Einstein came up with the basic idea in 1917, and the first working version was invented in 1960, by a scientist called Theodore Maiman.

Maiman made his laser by placing two mirrors opposite each other, with a ruby in between. A flash of light was shined onto the ruby, making it glow with red light. Some of this light shone onto one of the mirrors, which reflected it back through the ruby to the second mirror. It continued to be reflected between the two mirrors, each time getting brighter as it passed through the ruby. Finally, it escaped as a brilliant burst of red light—the world's first laser beam.

In 1960, no one knew what to do with lasers. They were called a "solution looking for a problem." But now they are used for all sorts of things, from eye operations to cutting through metal and measuring distances to a previously unheard-of accuracy.

3-second sum-up

Lasers make a new kind of entirely artificial light that is a powerful tool for industry and science.

An artificial Sun

The world's most powerful laser is in California. Its job is to crush tiny pellets containing the element hydrogen, which is the primary element of the Sun. The intense laser beam raises the temperature of the pellets to millions of degrees. The idea is to set off the same kind of nuclear reaction as the one that powers the Sun.

The light from a laser
is different from any kind
of natural light and can be
used in ways that no
other light can.

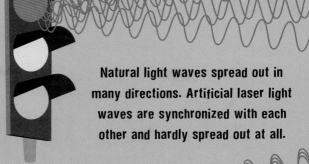

Natural light waves spread out in
many directions. Artificial laser light
waves are synchronized with each
other and hardly spread out at all.

Laser pen

There are four types of lasers, from
Class 1 (weakest) to Class 4 (most powerful).

Class 1:
CD and DVD players

Class 2:
Barcode readers

Class 3:
Light shows

Class 4:
Welding

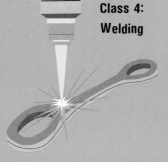

Robot

... in 30 seconds

During the 19th century, factories appeared all over the world, bringing with them jobs that were repetitive, boring, and often dangerous, too. The arrival of automatic machines improved things, but the problem with these machines was that they were built to do just one particular thing.

Then, in 1961, a new kind of machine started working in a car factory in New Jersey. Called Unimate, it could be programmed to do many different tasks—it was the world's first working robot. Robots share many characteristics with us; they have a brain (a computer); muscles (motors); senses (sensors) and a power source.

Today, many jobs—such as making cars or computers—are done almost entirely by robots. It's not just factories where robots have taken over from people. There are many jobs that robots can do better than we do, including space exploration, repairing underwater cables, bomb-disposal, and complicated surgery.

3-second sum-up

Robots can do many things better than we can.

3-minute mission Design a robot

1 First of all, decide what you want your robot to do—clean your room, do your homework, climb trees, walk the dog?

2 What kind of "actuators" (hands/arms) does your robot need—a built-in vacuum-cleaner? Tentacles? A lasso? Wheels?

3 How should your robot sense its surroundings? It's not limited to human senses—it could access wi-fi or have built-in radar.

4 Draw and label your invention. Remember you need to include a computerized brain and a source of power.

Robots are changing our lives. We can program them to do all kinds of useful jobs that are too dull or harmful for humans to do.

Spy robots use wi-fi to send sounds and images back to HQ.

Radio aerial

Camera

"Actuator" (hand) with self-adjusting grip

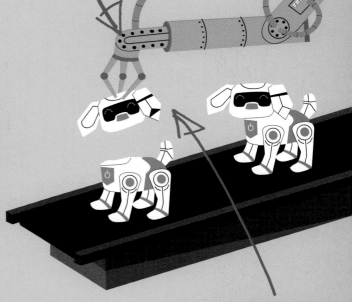

Drill, to search for underground life

The Curiosity Rover traveled 140 million miles (225,000 km) to explore Mars, and was able to make simple decisions to protect itself.

Assembly-line robot arms are fast, strong, and accurate.

Cleaning robot

Remote-control fire-fighting robot

Discover more

FICTION BOOKS

The Inventors by Alexander Gordon Smith and Jamie Webb
Faber and Faber, 2007

NON-FICTION BOOKS

1000 Inventions and Discoveries by Roger Bridgeman
Dorling Kindersley, 2014

1001 Inventions and Awesome Facts from Muslim Civilization by National Geographic
National Geographic Kids, 2013

Horribly Famous: Inventors and their Bright Ideas by Dr. Mike Goldsmith
Scholastic, 2010

Journal of Inventions: Leonardo Da Vinci by Jaspre Bark, David Hawcock, and David Lawrence
Silver Dolphin, 2009

Technology by Clive Gifford
Scholastic, 2012

The Story of Inventions by Anna Claybourne and Adam Larkum
Usborne Publishing Ltd., 2012

The Way Things Work by Chris Oxlade and Michael Harris
Lorenz Books, 2009

The What on Earth? Wallbook of Science & Engineering: A Timeline of Inventions from the Stone Ages to the Present Day by Christopher Lloyd and Andy Forshaw
What on Earth Publishing Ltd., 2013

DVDs — suitable for all ages

Wallace and Gromit's World of Invention (BBC, 2010)

WEBSITES

Advice about inventing
http://www.crackingideas.com/
Invention challenges and competitions, activity packs, and games.

Industrial Revolution
http://science.howstuffworks.com/innovations/inventions/5-industrial-revolution-inventions.htm
Top ten Industrial Revolution inventions.

Inventions in History
http://www.history.com/topics/inventions
News, videos and games about inventions past and present.

Science inventions
http://www.sciencekids.co.nz/sciencefacts/scientists.html
Facts about famous scientist inventors; elsewhere on the site there's information about robots, the Internet, space, and more.

Stories of inventors
http://invention.smithsonian.org/centerpieces/iap/inventors_main.html
Famous and lesser-known inventors' stories.

Victorian inventions
http://primaryhomeworkhelp.co.uk/victorians/inventions.htm
Timeline of Victorian inventions, from the first photograph to Marconi's radio.

APPS

Journeys of Invention by the Science Museum, 2013
Explore more than 80 world-famous scientific inventions.

Index

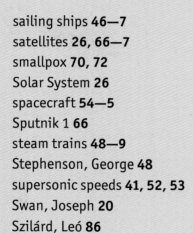